Solecism
poems by Rosebud Ben-Oni

Virtual Artists Collective
vacpoetry.org
ISBN 978-0-944048-50-4

Grateful acknowledgment is made to the editors of the following journals in which these poems first appeared, some in different form or with different titles: *Amethyst Arsenic:* Selections from "Shoal"; *Arts & Letters:* "X"; *The Bakery:* "For the Mixed Child with Pale Skin"; *Confrontation:* "Proof of Absence"; *CURA:* "Over the River from Sal Si Puedes"; *DMQ Review:* "After a Funeral in Jerusalem"; *Existere:* "Khamseen"; *The Fox Chase Review:* "Off the Q"; *Generations Literary Journal:* "A Poem for My Niece on No Particular Day"; *The Golden Triangle:* "At Ten at I had the Look of Locust" and "So Grows the Tree"; *J Journal:* "The Current Political Situation of the Roma"; *Maggid:* Selections from "Shoal"; *Niche Magazine:* "Crossing in Brazier Fumes" and "Call Her Ishtar"; *Off the Coast* : "Palms of Lebanon"; *Poecology:* "Gangster as Narwahl" and "Pauraque"; *Poydras Review:* "*Agunah*"; *Puerto del Sol:* "Song of Waxing Gibbous"; *The Rialto:* "The Youth"; *Stone Highway Review:* Selections from "Shoal"; *Tidal Basin Review:* "Coming of Age in Sal Si Puedes," "Creation Story of Sal Si Puedes" and "The Reply of Sal Si Puedes"; *Third Wednesday:* "Loving a Woman in Jerusalem," "Lives of Carrion" and "Crop Dusting in The Desert"

The cover painting is by Rogelio "El Indio" Cisneros. The cover design is by Regina Schroeder (forgetgutenberg.com). The text is set in Goudy Bookletter 1911.

To Robin, Olivera, Kristen, Bob, Andy and Anthony

and for my parents

CONTENTS

SOLECISM

1 nonstandard or ungrammatical usage
2 breach of good manners or etiquette
3 any error, impropriety or inconsistency

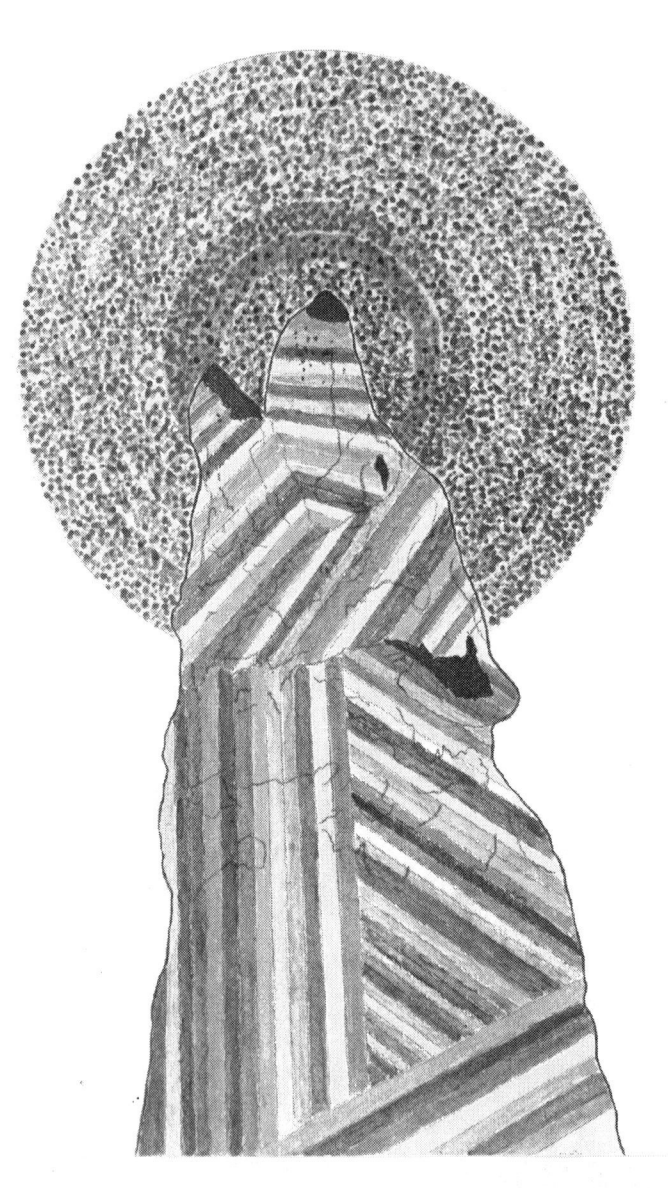

At Ten I Held the Look of Locust

At ten, I held the look of locust and mothers of tarp and tin
        held closer their unborn in the streets of childpits.

At ten, the Americans came and built a factory for the women
        to work with solvents and a playground for their children.

In August I'd roost on the sheetmetal roof as a bad omen:
        that lazy locust should be devastating fields.

But nothing ever grew in the *colonia.* My devastation, unsimple:
        A pain to say when not plural, shameful place among pests.

I held the look of locust, black-sunken eyes and long, thin limbs
        so mothers of melting plastic and plywood

scrambled for sawdust from the mouths of razor-wild men.
        Bloody nails wrote the mornings after in pencil lead.

I was unborn again, casting the look of locust, leather-rebellious nymph,
        swarming in constant omission, twitching in sin.

Twenty years later, the factory is condemned, but the playground stands
        with a sign in English: *WARNING: Toxic waste, no playing.*

Twenty years later, I am dust and molted locust skins.
I look through the fine webbing, yellow vapor
of the never-born, swinging windless, all limb.

Coming-of-Age in Sal Si Puedes[1]

—Baghdad Beach, Matamoros, Mexico

Even the gulls scuttled from the surf:
a grey arm erect and bit of shoulder
wrapped in electrical wire—

Workers hanging from scaffolds of a patiobar
spotted the waves scattering the next body.
This one, a Brownsville journalist

tied up in a metal drum and doused
with slow-burning gasoline.
We lit our sparkles and sang:

Do not fall out of the panga,
when the coyote asks you to make room—
The waters are cold and the guns carry

more weight than you.
Wind chipped a glare
in the carrousels, its scalloped mirrors

---

[1]   Sal Si Puedes means "Leave if you can" and is not an uncommon name for *colonias* and other neighborhoods found in the United States and Latin America.

full of bloodless faces and fists,
matted hair in the combers.
The police let their man

submerge into a carnival scene.
Only we are not afraid and watch him
watching us in that endless circling:

Senoritas kissing between lights spark
carnivorous noises of animal rhymes,
to have, to hunt, yawning lion

sack of burlap
to the once-bitten lamb
with the succubus grin.

δ

Undying is spinning backwards,
sand in my rubberbanded hair,
bitter traces of five-star pool.

At dawn he drips wax to preserve me.
Rawboned, delicate angles
bent by our heat.

Razors graze my hollows
for his perfect line. I sear
until I'm rosy as a daiquiri.

Tonight I fish-hook the eyes of other men.
Our son will come-of-age as Corinthian leather
and shoes and starched and the Sunday edition.

δ

I awaken on a mound of sand

and demand a manenough to bring
shaved ice and a shot glass.

He jumps from the railing as my sandals
fly off, the jellyfish outlining beer bottles.

The surf slides toward our briar mound.
His boots are wet, my bare feet fall away.

Shells gather like cemetery flowers.
A warning from where mermaids
siesta in the shark's atrium.

Creation Story of Sal Si Puedes

hanging off street corners
lamps lighting the last kerosene

accessible as the savage wants
howling girl
against a narcotic wire
the next rush
against
shift-changing bell

musket-chained born middle-aged
the last migrant and virgin widow

sterile   absent
legless in legacy

foothold found none

foolish to hold onto things

Over the River from Sal Si Puedes

girls grow slowly here
in greying eyelet dresses
under molted mocking birds

outside in rocking chairs
we mark time in losing it
even the eagle, a widow

shed from distant high winds,
has forgotten continuous flight
inseparable from the horizon

a promise has been broken
under junipers camphor lingers
the only pioneers, strangers

δ

they cross without shame
sway like young cattails,
swarm mosquitos and matted beds
of water hyacinth and hydrilla

we awaken with pond in our legs

they swim in the sulphurous lake
wrapped up in water moccasins
their grandmother was our mothers' keeper,

      howling in distant *guaje* trees,
      by lanterns outside a damaged Cathedral

      she baptized her daughters in rainwater,
      and razed her husband, the ashes
      fed to our mothers in molasses

      so we are more dust
      than embers, more moss than men
      at night we hear a new truck in the distance,

      her laughter burns bright eternal poinsettias
      weeds overrun our ranches
      seagulls loom over drought land

she will be the last
we will stomp her out yet
we will stomp her out yet

The Reply of Sal Si Puedes

I am the mistress of fragmentation.
Vestige of what's allowable but
Hardly livable.
Mosaic of outlander passings.

My ruins and limbs are
Parvenu to be archaic.
Autistic to partake in restoration.
Novel but not like neon-plated
Tijuana, a *peso* who thinks herself a penny.

Can't be museumed.
History skips over my life.

Confused that I speak intelligently?
Think the pinched aren't polysyllabic?

What if I said
Shall?
What if I experience—
Linguistic momentum
to earn Webster worth?
Would you call it broken then
in its 4th edition?

What say my tongue—
Blade rusted from stabbing
where I pick my teeth—
My cells are degenerates, no?

Guess how many lives *I* have.
Tear me down again—
I'll grease rouge on my wounds.
I was born with clothes
ripped in the right places.

I'm not a prophet for the world.
I wear the loin-cloth for self-loathing
purpose.
Won't speak in tongues.

I lost my lips to a tracker long ago.

I'm not a foreshadow of the divine.
Quit photographing my children for
exposés of The Second Coming.
I'm sleepwalking through your Op-Eds.
I am not in your worldly terms.

Your first word was remembered.
I was born a *muerto*.
You—
Have yet to let me finish a sentence.

For the Mixed Child with Pale Skin

You'll never be comfortable with the purist and the insurgent,
        when called porcelain

by Gifted and Talented teachers who appropriate what you say.
        A step away from the nasty

bits, some say you gentrify the ghettos of the canon.
        Whitewash over the boredom of limited choices,

the Other that no one will claim, your parts don't look
        the part in anything.

If you're pretty, consider the patronage of nature
        but never the sparrow,

tough, little plebian. No—pose with macaw on shoulder,
        draw out the exotic, threat of large beak

near your delicate, not quite-white. That's how dangerous
        is loved, that's friendly ethnic.

But now you've offended by writing this. You have to be careful
        in conferences by ethnicities you half

belong to. Nothing sings how there is never unity for you.
        Turn not to your parents: love still blindsides them.

By the way you look off with a cool haircut
        so you can never be a hipster,

always too sexy-off-the-shoulder
        even in suits—your mentor interrupts: writing

this makes you rather juvenile. She tells you race
        is no longer taboo. She has won major prizes and disdains

your poems about a Mexican border town,
        where she got drunk and bought pain pills during college.

You are her past—stories told in embarrassment.
        And yet adaptation has made you

like the sparrow—what is always suddenly,
        in the fray, stealing crumbs from larger birds,

devouring what it can in the chase,
        helpless to an unsightly candor.

Pauraque

I.

The love child of sparrows and curmudgeon trees,
how we envied their roots, dull and deep,
a massively braided tumor two feet
above ground—
it was all we could see
when we were children in the hurricane
how easily sparrows resettle and the pauraque
too among us, wings of dead leaves, hidden.

II.

The heart of a hatchling
is yellowed ivory, its eyes
hard currency, its tends toward
nullity, an unrepentant soul.

One day I too will disappear
into overflowing ashtrays and
stryofoam pyramids
in ten-peso shops.

III.

It has the ability to fly but prefers to run,
feed off the mosquitos of the river's edge.

Sirens sound and crush its fragile bones.
Its blood soaks my bare sole, and I do not
dare the river, I do not dare
the river.

Shoal

Tonight you die quiet and sudden in a dream,
God staggering through the Galapagos,
pinning the birds like brooches
as they twitter his nerves,
all that you knew
to be untrue
intangible as the blue base of a flame.

δ

In Hebrew School you could not hide
your mother's tongue, the trilling Rs
and dragging intonations from your Israeli
teacher Ziva who came from dirty, dusty Afula.

You were chosen
as Ester for the Passover play
because Ziva thought you a dark thing:

there was a woman in the caves of Ein Gedi,
who dresses as me during Passach.
Drowns my shibboleth in Elijah's cup.

15

She called you Ishtar and told you
goddesses don't have parents, only rivals.
She told you it takes an exile to endure another.

On stage you were allowed no lines,
a mute without a slate, hooded in all
black, a slit for eyes.
You marked time in
telluric Xs. Not a goddess
at the crossing, but the fool's
fool, opportunist, the dark horse
of maundering.

δ

Once you played a blind widow
on one leg in St. Luke's
surgical theater. Gangrene capped
your toes dropping off in green

Leggos lying in ruins, your wrecking-ball brother
abandons you on 2 am streets, sparrows sing

just beneath your sleep, the wind
howling down Dyckman.

You dream a passing procession,
you face the Virgin Guadalupe
on a poster, a voodoo doll, an urn of clay
covered in sweaty garland and grease.
Goat blood foams in the Hudson.

> You hopscotch barefoot
> outside Grant's tomb.
> The Virgin staring, the Ché staring,
> Buicks with megaphones—

You weep as the red-faced coachman strikes his horse,
absurd plume drooping, carriages looping
like cattle-cars over you,

> silent herald stuck on a lopsided stool
> stranded along Riverside in plastic sandals.
> Less than a pedestrian who fears
> red lights and bike messengers

speeding across Columbus Avenue,
always frostbitten and antique,
where scaffolds lash out
over rosewood shops and still startle you.

δ

Outside St. John the Unfinished, you scorn the sensible:
a miracle materialized on heartwood.
Paint peeling a child's face
restored from polio, from his mother's rosary

        hangs a broken neck—a saint's
        last performance, her primitive
        mouth howling over a casket,
        a compost bin.

You hear the stained-glass burst open,
its translucent doves impaled on a forklift.

Mistaking their aim, prongs have pierced
through and discovered you in a confessional.

δ

You are in a windy Lower East Side square.

Henry Street, arid and slow.
An elderly street without monuments.
Arched in inner city catheters
bending the sun. A contradiction but warm.

Crackling in exhaust fumes.

Cracking like Rivera's murals at the New School
where you write of the idolatry of the Wailing Wall
opaque and palpable.

You cross Brooklyn bridge.
A river a summons a cemetery
a howl cut short,
barb wire overcast.

> Pages scattering from a mausoleum,
> you fall out of its doorway, taken
> as sacrament. Useless vandal.
> Evicted tenant.

δ

You call yourself   an Annex Jew—

from the Frick's untouchable pools
sinking down
an upright bass on the Bowery

you and the pianist climb the terrace of Beatrice Inn

you are lost among long tables of refugees
and folk hymns muffled on Allen Street

Sabbath morning, coarse and whimsical
leaks its veil in Chinatown's oils

sober and lit without sleep
alone on a pier
the edge of Battery sharpens
pampas along the surf howl and stretch

here strikes your last prayer
a bruised howl in the wall
and oh, to sleep
to sleep through

the brute of dawn

Call Her Ishtar

—For Mike Wexler

When night was an octave lower,
and our eyes owl-wide,

when love struck along the bass line
and we cried *forte, fortissimo*

four hours before sunrise--
When our unease had no grief,

and pretenders saved us again on Purim eve
as Haredim fluttered down *Mea Sharim,*

before this rueful heart played its last card,
before rimshots ended those high AM hours,

your right hand coming
to teal down the footlights,

        I believed in the morning star

    giving way to a wonder
    as simple and young as us
    sliding in our socks

below a carillon of waking birds
and rain, as drawing the first weevil
from the cracks.

Agunah[2]

In absentia, he holds—you,
tichel-crumpled, bare-legged
and humbled, shown your hair
in the *shuq*, shorn of husband.

Alone, the *shuq* is a sudden holding:
Flies and bees abandon the sweets seller.
Fish leap, cut open themselves
at your feet. Who sways behind you,

but the kind of men who pluck them
from the dust and still hawk
sloppy-fleshed, the blood
already too many days old.

How long can the faded-rose gills
hold that last gasp,
long enough to read such dull eyes,
past their prime and most peculiar?

---

[2]   A *halachic* term for a woman who, in this case, has been abandoned by her
husband.

X

Sharon proposes another date—February 21st—
I'm not sure how to prepare for it,
so we arise early in our flat on Givat Tsarfatit.

Outside, we recycle our empty plastics.
The communal white vans, the catcalls follow—
I must prepare myself—
yet open air markets
and sunroofs have sated me
for a stretch of life. This walk
to the one back are sedative.
At the grocer's doors, the guard searches us
with only *boker tov.*

That only happens when I'm with you, she accuses.

Somewhere we are mobilizing against mass destruction.

I investigate the firmness of melons
though she chooses the first ones I touch.
Bananas with a few brown spots,
the tart oranges. This yogurt keeps
until tomorrow, I tell her. And on sale,

sabras[3], prickly pears.

Not all the spines were removed,
and she inspects my hand
as if it will turn against me.
We find splinters from the bed frame
and yet I feel little—
it must be the frozen food—
a blue undertow flows beneath my palm.

Will it come while I'm looking for bargains?

Am I ready? Am I proud?

Eat something, Amina pays again,
instead of delusion eating you.

At home, I shower instead.
Water so hot my skin blisters
and begs, my skeleton clattering
like picked bones on a plate.

---

3   A sabra is also another word for a native-born Israeli.

Proof of Absence

—Mount Scopus, an Israeli enclave in Arab East Jerusalem

People who I don't know at all
ask me what it's like to survive
a bombing. They are shocked

to hear it is like bad music
I can't get out of my head.
That it was not more meaningful

or made my words unforgettable.
At 3 a.m. I arise and chance the roads,
lurk behind the cemented-up windows

of his voided home. The newborn
flailing in the exiled mother's arms.
I meet the anger in the eyes

of his son, later captured
on a Human Rights website.
I do not go to the trial,

nothing cannot be returned
to us, much less them.
Nor do these lines

lead to the dead.
Rather, to their martyrdom
outliving the living.

But even these are not facts.

The Youth

Nothing new to report: charred clothing
for the photographers. Same poses, faces

escaping the light as it showed its face,
a lesser sun. Upclose, its true nature

would bring ruin—this same patron of life
when millions of miles away.

It took a youth to go back into the burning house,
and fall out of the smoke with the Arab.

It took a youth to hide his other arm
that was nearly no longer there

from the anger that swarmed to a pause.
Disorder—not feeling—returned the crowd

to their heads. They sorted the wounded,
choosing to sidestep the young man

and his charge. He did not cry out
a fragile masterpiece

picked up on the BBC that night.
He, natural as a father,

ushered the Arab into an ambulance,
slamming its doors on her gown

and then stooped off into the street.
No one called after him, after

        pieces of him
        out-of-camera shot
        found their way into a stretcher,
        Mourner's Kaddish, some say,
        opening his lips.
        But for who?

No one thought to ask.

After a Funeral in Jerusalem

I.

Shiva is three nights at Haoman 17:
you climb the shoulders of an *echis*
commander, and claw
at the high ceiling. In the morning

you skid across the cafés of King Solomon.
In the light it is your face the young mourn.
Behind the cracked mirror of an old compact,
you throw your voice to order *cafe hafuch*,

for you stand too close to the edge.

II.

Women in White are protesting
Women in Black protesting
in Zion Square, calling for the end of *people*
not a people and *castle builders in the desert.*

Each wants strike open a gate
of water from her stone.
You want to lie in each of her arms
and be that only child,

a single cell born in the Dead Sea.

III.

You break into Yemin Moshe
to sleep in the cold gazebo.
Its roses have little to offer—
That is why you've come

to expect them at any hour.
You are not the first to break
into restricted areas

wanting nothing at all.

Khamseen[4]

On the other side
of the sealed window

the hooves of the donkey
stammer in the *khamseen*.

We hear the tall, spare man
bellow, and the shrill answer, *neigh*,

neigh. Their voices scatter
in the swelling dust.

I tap quietly on the window,
useless as the elderly animal

who ran out to unburden
all involved. But their cries

continue, even after the faint sun
goes out. The wind raps harder

---

[4]   A rather intense dusty storm that descends yearly upon the Middle East
and North Africa.

on the window. Cursing the man,
you turn away and fall asleep.

I listen well into the night,
envying that donkey.

Crossing in Brazier Fumes

Before one dawn of Ramadan
we finally unroofed the room.

Inebriated on hunger,
Left scrawl-spoken—

> *Slowly, slowly,* you let in some air.
> My head hurts from the brazier fumes.

I speak low
from the ground, toss
out the silence.

Here's a trick in English:
The sound of me
in Hebrew means "who"
& who is "he" & he is "she"—

> *I can't understand.* Half your body is in Ramallah,
> a woman in the window, three-quarter-sleeves

> the other half inside a quarter-queer
> shaking on thin, bare legs.

Dawn, expressionless
and always punctual,

belittles the chronicles of these houses.

Your back heaves from the window,
the voice of a *sheik* buzzing behind you.

> A casual scratch behind the hand:
> *Let's go before the sun comes up.*

You dress quickly, will fast like a martyr
for another day and ace the oral with a blank face

> while silently cursing us in your own language.

> *Who is He is She?*

At the first check-point,
I suck the rage you left on my tongue.

Loving a Woman in Jerusalem

I.

Quit the body for awhile. Upped the air
in a gamble until the *khamseen* swept me aside,

and left all hanging. You were the child clapping
erasers, choking on my mistakes, to please the teacher.

II.

Night has become a kind of field dress.

A stranger stretching the iron
frame and we bend and bend

into a farther upon we cannot depend on.

III.

No partaking of a cigarette, no faint words.
Only the drawing of steel
back around your shoulders.

IV.

In the corner of my eye, always a rat's tail,
a extra step in the staircase, phantom shadows.

But it is the blind spots holding together
these last scraps of crowds and carbon.

V.

Dancer's pivot,
the illusion of ease
balancing on a block of wood,

of hands wanting only a waist, a face-off
between sequins and a spotlight that does not burn.

The Current Political Situation of the Roma

There is progress, yes.
There are scholars and lobbyists,
journalists, philanthropists and bigots—

Begins too vague.
That last word is unnecessary.

So edit out what you like.
The bottom line is...
there is a *returning* being built up:
erected, shining and...*poignant.*

Not quite sure about your tone here.
Do not be imprudent with italics.

Yes, yes, let's tear off the tentacles,
drain the crystal ball of its liquid smoke,
unleash the dancing bear into a crowd:
like a Gypsy, I am incapable of candor.

Do not generalize.

At least I capitalized the G,
but here's a specific example.

My grandfather's father
was in demand
as a luxury hotel waiter
because tourists believed he looked
the most "Spanish" of Spaniards.
Such a pretender leaves behind a litter
of those incapable of candor.

> *"Litter" sounds derogatory.*
> *Personal narrative is unacceptable.*
> *AKA, avoid using first person.*

But then I can't pull a *hokkano baro*—

> *What does this mean? Needs a footnote!*

At least this time I was not imprudent with italics.
Why don't you look it up— *Wikipedia*, perhaps*?*

> *Not a source for college!*

Do your exclamation points
indicate displeasure? I learned
your words, but not you, mine?

> *Pardon? You are going off topic.*

I warned you:

I am incapable of candor.
And I'll *gyp* you any chance I can.

> *Moreover, why did you assume you could write a poem?*

Now I'm not sure about *your* tone, Professor.
Like people who subsist on oral tales,
history too is fertile, unsettled,
completely incapable of candor—

> *Historians rely on proof.*

—but I do have proof:

Now the ~~Gypsies~~ Rroma have a flag
with a red wheel upon green and blue.
There is talk of nation building
and our rights and some "right
to return" business.

> *Some centuries ago, India, it seems, threw you—*

away.

> *I was going to say "out of the country."*

Or perhaps they'd sent us to fight the Muslims
or sold some of us to a Wallachian tyrant
with a taste for Turkish spines on stakes.

But thank God, now those scholars and lobbyists,
journalists, philanthropists and bigots
all wish us a home.

Vague, again! Documents your sources.

You try digging us up from the ditches,
train stations and antique stores.
And yet we are very much here, aren't we,
multiplying like a plague
which drives you batty—

Second person is unacceptable.
Implicates the reader.

Wouldn't you miss our smug
suffering and faces to the wind
and ridiculous King of the Universe
crowning himself in pure gold
just as suggested in Gypsy Lore—

But it comes down to this:
someone has studied us
just enough
to find a promise land.

Once I walked on water

Faith wouldn't take away the "F" you're getting.

where faith rages and roves,
a hound without loving master,
leaving its footprints on anything
darkened with backfire and sewers.

Still no excuse for a paper written by hand.

Naturally. Who falls anymore
for these old tricks?

I cannot reward creativity.
Historians must be responsible.

I cannot be a historian.
We tell our stories by mouth only,
We do not hold our stories in such
Rigid restraints; if they change by another's
Tongue, we simply tell them again.

You're using "we" again—Unacceptable!

Fine: I too was born with a loose grip.
But have no fear:
My mother knew I was not hers to keep

I sense a sympathy ploy—though granted,
it's a step up from missing a train/train
stopped on the bridge excuse—

when I picked up the pencil
she left me,

the lines of my palm
navigating nowhere.

Lives of Carrion

Later, I'll tell them it was too dark
to see I was bleeding

while you searched for the shell casing
to show your superior.

She came just north of the Golan, showed
contempt for this contested frontier.

For months this low, creeping creature
squeezed past the road blocks and made off

with our chickens. Her smell of stagnant
waters marking our fence.

What was a jackal to a poet then
but the mistress of lackeys and squatters.

A plague on four legs. An over-grown sandfly,
carrier of cutaneous ulcers and Aleppo boils.

Tomorrow the former commander will toss aside
the casing, plod to his foothold in the vineyard.

But tonight the only sound is you.
I leave the wound open, and she

burrows closer. What will she leave behind,
perhaps a trail for her mate to find, is it true

that Beirutis still long to recover
years after returning to Lebanon,

while the Syrian troops forgot the provisional
walls of their compounds and remain.

I fear the day we reap
the hour in being forgotten,

seek warmth from the ones
who take it away. Tomorrow he'll find us

and rip apart the henhouse. You say the cripple
who coaxes errant vines up the trellis

once led a tank battle in these fields.
For now all is quiet in the North.

I let her bite once more.
A nudge of teeth and spittle-blood,

falling warm into my own.
Later, I'll peel the scab over,

wanting to scar, and try to tell
time from patches on the ground.

Palms of Lebanon

a lull in war
the last trunks mourn
new bullet thorns

gulls fly out to the Pigeon Rocks
emerge with barnacles of smoke

in Nablus your uncle sells you *sus*
glasses clinking at his belt
blistering bitterness

in Gaza City they buy inflatable Yasser Arafats
not able to stand upright like you,
man of lank

your aerial turning into a perfect
cartwheel, your hands coming down
to the ground at the last moment

branches flip their swords at the planes

tomorrow uproots that stagnant
heel stranded in mud

tomorrow bends in the head
and burning sea

Crop-dusting in the Desert

I.

Stiffly, in iambs: the stir of wing
And then darkness burning in the wind.

II.

Ripples in dunes: ruin without ruin. Scorpion
and nomad like weeds weathering the cracks.

III.

Even the birds have gone suicidal: the cracked body
a pyre, lusting to die. From ashes, a storm of poison.

IV.
Only the locust does not fail the unseen
seed, inseparable from the undergrowth of a wadi.

V.
Five pairs of strings, now you tune your broken oud,
Away from the false bird that cares not what it burns.

(don't call it returning)

—JFK Airport, New York, 2007

sometimes all sound
seems ramble in bramble
jet-fueled not known of humble

left full-lipped caught on gums
muffled, miffed
pigeon dissonance

trial of pin-feather trail, riled
deplumed and shed of guided hound

I lost
Jerusalem
(was, in)

now riding the 7
exposed train tracks
Corona, Elmurst, Last Stop
Flushing
I want to believe my silence

what I met in the eye of storm
where the point of the spiral
beginning all

What Lies at the End of Long-Distance

In still streetlamp-lit morning,
after the second sleepless night,
I believe in songless birds
bellowing
exposed
train track
graffiti—

What I've failed I will not unknow.
What has failed me is not yet unknown.

On the Q33
I sit close to the driver
as if I'll miss your terminal,
as if the airport harbors only departures

I am a songless bird
only unstrange in waiting rooms,
all the never-to-be relics
what travels as the pass-through
loose threads
ramshackle cargo

I'm a songless bird
sitting on a dirty conveyor belt
in baggage claim

The light is blinking,
the belt warming up
as you weave
through a mob of drivers
dressed in Sunday finest

we grab hold among those
holding up signs for strangers

So Grows the Tree

I am not gentle with names.
Leung: swell of throat, an almost not
touching the tongue
across the roof   you say
it means central supporting
beam, holding up
the house
we were building

I come from a sullen coast
where trees die twigs
exposed brittle white and burnt
makeshift tarp tin
homes easily almost not
easily left
I grew in the not discerning
double negative correct
fanned my headdress to invite
the hurricanes   tagged
my voice in the swell
adrift
in leaving

I am not gentle with names.

Leung: how waves rise, holding
when known
only to themselves   only
to ourselves it is not spoken
it is always
almost, and leaves
as the before of a kiss
constant but not continuing
as bending the thick
feeling of swelling

wandering the wreck
we pull at plyboard and lost timber

I must find from where it came.
only then I will not be adrift
only then as the twig isn't bent

Quarrel of Sparrows

One early morning, dull, brown shells
skip, feet together,
sullen in infinite pucker.

How close they are,
always,
to the end.
Forever, a cold winter day not unlike today.

I purse my lips and shiver:
This bench is not forever.

Today is always, is what I meant.
Food, flock, nest, is what I meant.

I'm envious. Sometimes I waste the day
digging through dead leaves.

I will never know
forever,
or sense something before it happens,

and so they fly away, breaking
my heart on this cold, cold day.

The True Bird Lover

I.

The true bird lover knows the calls
and remains skeptical—

maybe a mynah on the loose,
domestic deviant
hobbling in tall grass,
spewing housework gunshots

the fabled wilderness of Charlton Heston
babysitter scraping Teflon
Aflac duck

II.

Wild amazons kiss the caged
in our chain-fence yards

we post NO STANDING ANY TIME
and pamphlets of immigration laws

they are our overlords
mimicking innocence
post-pioneer

III.

not a witness, the lover engages
can't sit still
has to interrupt—
the bird watchers' nightmare

she's just as fed-up
as the errant penguin in the Herzog film

can't explain
her particular kind
to her kind collective

that lone running toward
indistinct distance

mountains of ice
more alive
breaking grief
and nominal silence

The Gangster as Narwhal

You woo the circulating blades
of a motor's *whoop-whoop, whoop,*

those eyes of a puritan courting
with a swivel-chain woe.

You capsized my slender boat,
with your horn, the only means of teeth

spiraling still—how well you play a drowned
corpse, my deep diver, far from swan-spined

or supple-sighted. Your song in the dark
is discordant: the reeling-in of broken

lines, the echo of a lost howl, prehistoric
falling, the suddenness of a shot in the dark.

Off the Q

Did I taste a toadstool
sitting in a white-walled room
off Lincoln and Ocean Avenue,

where the trains no longer keep me awake
passing by below, open and exposed,
the sharp sound of metal and voltage

like a grace note off a drum roll,
the snare head loose and low.
The blinds have never been gentle

with the dawn, the harsh glare
stabbing through like an evangelist
jumping up and down to move

millions. But when I needed hell-fire most,
in the late morning, especially on Shabbat
when I shouldn't be writing at all,

The light fades to rubbish gray,
and the Q train shakes my solid desk,
the canopy bed—even the floors creak

and shift in protest. Yet I love the lobby
too large and impractical, its yearly
winter gash of a collapsed

floor from above. Then there's the super's boys
who pretend to be *muy padre* when my ceiling
comes loose and the outlets are falling out of the wall.

I'm scared to change the bulb
in the bathroom fixture, it requires
four hands minimum and a kamikaze spirit.

There are the boys whose father sits outside
in a wheelchair late on school nights
and twice a year he's risen

to give a shake-down to those
who've dared to follow me home.
Teenage girls hang near the tiny mailboxes

that hold nothing, until the grandmas
come over with their laundry carts
and tell them they'd better get to school,

or they'll always be in this falling apart
and given to leak. Bumper stickers on a 2nd floor
front door proclaims "Jesus loves you"

and across the building lies Prospect Park
where swans stretch their spines in indifference,
enormous trees and the clearest of skylines.

Even deep within I hear the rumble of the train,
and for that reason I'm moved to believe
that Jesus might very well love me,

a Jew who writes on the Sabbath,
as another train rolls in,
though more faintly.

I'm still waiting
for what grows in broken concrete
among the weeds and jagged ends.

Dabar

new neighbors button
their beliefs to "Occupy,"
boast "100% Cruelty-Free"
while blasting their music weekday nights

in our working-class building, they mock
my super's accent, not understanding

he lost some of his jaw to cancer,
when he wants them to stop

vomiting in the hallway,
1 - 5 a.m. wasted
songs of protest, off-key Jimi Hendrix

when we call 311, they egg our doors at random

      I never want to speak 99%
      for my own behalf

      I will wipe down every door
      while they are still out there

      take the last eggs

so life unripened
does not fall to waste
but survives
the promise of rounded hand

A Poem for My Niece on No Particular Day

So here's to you, to the smudged, unsettled
paths you'll leave behind, to paint that never
dries, to new ground along old fault lines,
pause, and then—cross the blinding
dunes, defy the breach of a search
light, imbibe the screams of sea
clattering for you—
Know those incurable
depths, but know you cannot clean your room
by disappearing under the bed. So here's to asking
WHY—then WHY a second time
with the look of lion, to mornings that sound the burnished
pipes of an organ, to the daddy-long-legs over the summer
humming drains, to love as honest as spare change
found in a payphone, to last candles, to your first love, that fog
of the finest gossamer, may you find your way through it,
to Roman numerals a beloved carves into trees,
may you find the wise women beneath them,
to your late-in-the-evening, to skeptics you will meet,
may you be more April than Spring, may you unstitch the seams
of sentences, and from them know eternity,
ebbing and endless, crown of light, as you sing
the day—into night.

Song of Waxing Gibbous

—After Karla Kuskin's "Spring"

I'm uncoiling from coat pockets.
I'm undoing the no-take-backs,
When sky pranks a canopy of crows
Under exposed train tracks.
I'm shotgun on the raised platform.
I'm sailing towards.
I'm harboring daffodils.
I'm a lychee peel in peril
Plates tipping off the table
By catnipped paw.
I'm those ecstatic missing thumbs.
I'm ghosting the trains until home.
I'm a wash-and-wear sunburnt mess of curls.
I'm 7 Train Love Local,
No names Express
Third-rail rushing past,
Adults with childish faces
Triumphant at our marooned station.
I'm the *siesta* songless bird.
I sing swinging-tire unseemly.
Recuerda our knee-tall tagging,
Off the sullen coast?
I sing still you, Monito, underfoot in sand.

I sing still locust-looking, tin-roof-perching
Matarose.

7 Train Love

I'm grateful for the women in VIDA: Women in Literary Arts, and New Perspectives Theater, especially Melody Brooks. Mitch E. Parker, writer and editor extraordinaire, is a wonderful mentor as well as friend.

Leana, Mike, Matt, Sarah and Jordi were the first New York; poet Mark Rudman, the first inspritation. Ava and Jen got me through those hard Michigan winters.

In the home of Aimee and Scott Coleman, I often took refuge; your family is an inspiration.

Thanks to my parents and their families, my brother and his family.

Bakar and Cheri, I hear a certain "–Girl" is looking for you; still so many margaritas to drink together.

All the 7 Train Love in the world to whom this book is dedicated: Olivera, Kristen, Andy, Bob and Anthony.

Layla would not be without Lalo. Marian Haddad, my sister. Mason and Julia, another home.

I completed the final revisions of this book in Hong Kong on a stunning rooftop room of the home of Christina and Isaac Lee. Grateful for their kindness and generous nature, and showing me around the city. Grateful for their son Brian, my love, my light.

And where would I be without Robin Regina Ford? Probably somewhere lost in Drake's Eyebrows. Or watching good horror films. Now to find you a real Pomeraster.

Born to a Mexican mother and a Jewish father, Rosebud Ben-Oni is a graduate of the Women's Work Lab playwright at New Perspective Theater; her plays have been produced in New York City, Washington DC and Toronto. Winner of both the Seth Barkas Prize for Poetry and Thomas Wolfe Prize for Best Poetry Collection while an undergrad at New York University, she was a Rackham Merit Fellow at the University of Michigan and a Horace Goldsmith Scholar at the Hebrew University of Jerusalem. She is also co-editor for "HER KIND," the official blog of "VIDA: Women in Literary Arts". She lives in New York City. Find her at rosebudbenoni.com.

CPSIA information can be obtained at www.ICGtesting.com
Printed in the USA
BVOW040449250213

313919BV00001B/1/P